PORTRAITS OF THE STATES

★ ★

WASHINGTON, D.C.

by Geoffrey M. Horn

GARETH**STEVENS**

A Member of the WRC Media Family of Companies

Please visit our web site at: www.garethstevens.com
For a free color catalog describing Gareth Stevens Publishing's
list of high-quality books and multimedia programs, call
1-800-542-2595 (USA) or 1-800-387-3178 (Canada).
Gareth Stevens Publishing's fax: (414) 332-3567.

Library of Congress Cataloging-in-Publication Data

Horn, Geoffrey M.
    Washington, D.C. / Geoffrey M. Horn.
      p. cm. — (Portraits of the states)
    Includes bibliographical references and index.
    ISBN 0-8368-4676-1 (lib. bdg.)
    ISBN 0-8368-4695-8 (softcover)
    1. Washington (D.C.)—Juvenile literature. I. Title. II. Series.
    F194.3.H67   2006
    975.3—dc22   2005044474

This edition first published in 2006 by
Gareth Stevens Publishing
A Member of the WRC Media Family of Companies
330 West Olive Street, Suite 100
Milwaukee, WI 53212 USA

This edition copyright © 2006 by Gareth Stevens, Inc.

Editorial direction: Mark J. Sachner
Project manager: Jonatha A. Brown
Editor: Catherine Gardner
Art direction and design: Tammy West
Picture research: Diane Laska-Swanke
Production: Jessica Morris and Robert Kraus

Picture credits: Cover, © Corel; pp. 4, 21, 26 © Mae Scanlan; p. 5 © PhotoDisc;
pp. 6, 8, 9 © MPI/Getty Images; p. 10 © Mathew Brady Collection/Time & Life
Pictures/Getty Images; p. 11 © Library of Congress; p. 12 © Robert W. Kelley/
Time & Life Pictures/Getty Images; pp. 15, 22 © Gibson Stock Photography;
pp. 16, 20 © Don Eastman; pp. 24, 27 © Joe Raedle/Getty Images; p. 25 © Win
McNamee/Getty Images; p. 28 © Jerome Delay/AFP/Getty Images; p. 29 © Dave
Gillum/Diamond Images/Getty Images

Printed in the United States of America

1 2 3 4 5 6 7 8 9 10 09 08 07 06

CONTENTS

Chapter 1 Introduction 4

Chapter 2 History 6

Time Line 13

Chapter 3 People 14

Chapter 4 The Land 18

Chapter 5 Economy 22

Chapter 6 Government 24

Chapter 7 Things to See and Do 26

Glossary 30

To Find Out More 31

Index 32

Words that are defined in the Glossary appear
in **bold** the first time they are used in the text.

On the Cover: The Capitol stands at the heart of Washington, D.C.

Introduction

Washington, D.C., is an exciting place to visit. What would you like to see there? The house where the president lives? The Washington Monument? The National Zoo?

These places are famous. Perhaps you have seen pictures of them in books or on television. They are much more exciting when you see them up close.

Washington, D.C., is the nation's **capital**. Powerful people live there. They work for the U.S. government. The city also has beautiful parks and wonderful museums. You can learn about history, take walks, ride a bike, or enjoy a picnic in the city. There is always something to see and do in Washington, D.C.

Flowering cherry trees bloom in springtime near the Jefferson Memorial.

The flag of Washington, D.C.

WASHINGTON, D.C., FACTS

- Became the U.S. Capital: 1800
- Population (2004): 553,523
- Size: 61 square miles (158 square kilometers)
- Nickname: D.C.
- Tree: Scarlet oak
- Flower: American Beauty rose
- Bird: Wood thrush
- Motto: *Justitia Omnibus* (Justice for All)
- Song: "The Star-Spangled Banner," words by Francis Scott Key
- **Important Note**: Washington, D.C. is not a state. Also, it does not belong to any state. It is a "district" that stands alone as the capitol of the United States.

5

History

Native Americans were the first people to live in the area of Washington, D.C. A group called the Piscataway had a large village nearby in Maryland. They also had about thirty smaller villages. The Natives built their homes of bark. They fished in the Potomac River. They grew corn and pumpkins.

The English Arrive

English settlers came to Virginia in the early 1600s. Captain John Smith was their leader. He sailed up the Potomac River and met with the Piscataway. The meeting went well.

Later meetings were much less happy. The English settlers wanted the Natives' land. Other Native groups wanted the

This map of Washington, D.C., was made in 1880.

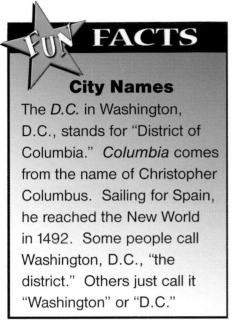

land, too. Many Piscataway died in battle. Others died of diseases they caught from the settlers.

A Nation Is Born

Many years passed. More settlers came to the New World. By the mid-1700s, Britain held thirteen **colonies** along the East Coast. Before long, the colonists became tired of British rule. They wanted to be free.

Britain did not want to let the colonies go. Britain and the colonies began to fight. In 1775, the Revolutionary War began. It lasted for eight years. The colonists won the war and won their freedom. The colonies became the United States.

New Nation, New Capital

By 1789, the nation had a **Congress** to make the laws. It also had a president to carry out the laws. But, the leaders had not yet chosen a city to be the capital of the new nation.

Congress took action in 1790. It passed a law that

IN WASHINGTON, D.C.'S HISTORY

Swamp
Before 1800, the capital was mostly swamp. Roads were bad. Buildings were few. Mosquitoes were everywhere. It took a lot of work to turn Washington, D.C., into a city!

Famous People of Washington, D.C.

Benjamin Banneker

Born: November 9, 1731, Baltimore County, Maryland

Died: October 19, 1806, Baltimore County, Maryland

Benjamin Banneker was the free son of freed slaves. He had little schooling. Even so, he read a lot and was very good at math.

Banneker worked as a farmer. He loved to go to his fields at night. There, he watched the stars and charted their positions. In 1791, he was asked to help lay out the new capital. He **surveyed** the land on which Washington, D.C., now stands.

set up a new capital. The capital would be built near the Potomac River.

Grand Plans

In 1791, George Washington was president. He asked Pierre L'Enfant to plan the new city. L'Enfant was French. He knew the great cities of Europe. He wanted the capital of the United States to be a great city, too.

L'Enfant planned a city with wide streets. The **Capitol** building was at the center of the city. The U.S. Congress moved into the Capitol in 1800.

Two Wars

The United States and Britain went to war again in 1812. Troops from Britain attacked Washington, D.C., in 1814. They set fire to

FUN FACTS

Not His Home Town

George Washington never lived in the city that has his name. He died in 1799. The city was not called Washington until after his death. The first president to live here was John Adams. He came in 1800. At first, his home was called the "President's House." Later, it became known as the **White House**.

the White House and the Capitol. A sudden thunderstorm saved both buildings. The heavy rains put out the flames.

Fifty years later, another war almost tore the country apart. The Civil War was fought between 1861 and 1865. A key issue was slavery. The southern states wanted to keep slavery. The northern states wanted to ban it.

Abraham Lincoln was the president during this time.

British troops attacked Washington, D.C., in 1814.

In 1862, he ended slavery in Washington, D.C. Then, thousands of escaped slaves moved into the city. They had run away from their owners in the South.

The war brought other changes to Washington, D.C. The Capitol was used as a hospital. Many wounded soldiers were treated there.

Years of Growth

The North won the Civil War in 1865. Slavery was banned all over the country. After the war ended, many buildings and **monuments** were built in Washington, D.C. New universities opened. Museums opened, too. The city was growing and changing.

Famous People of Washington, D.C.

Clara Barton

Born: December 25, 1821, North Oxford, Massachusetts

Died: April 12, 1912, Glen Echo, Maryland

Clara Barton believed in equal rights for women. When she worked as a teacher, she asked for the same pay as men. She lived in D.C. when the Civil War broke out. During the war, she worked as a nurse. She saved the lives of wounded soldiers. In 1881, she became the leader of the American Red Cross. She helped many families recover from war, floods, and other disasters.

IN WASHINGTON, D.C.'S HISTORY

The Night Lincoln Was Shot

On the night of April 14, 1865, Abraham Lincoln left the White House. He went to Ford's Theater to see a play. While he sat and watched, he was shot in the back of the head. He died the next morning. His killer was John Wilkes Booth. Booth had sided with the slave states in the Civil War. He died in a fight with U.S. troops on April 26.

More and more, people asked the U.S. government to solve problems in the nation. One problem was that African Americans were treated badly. They were not slaves, but they did not have the same rights as whites. In the mid-1900s, they began to demand equal treatment.

In 1963, more than 200,000 people crowded onto the National Mall. They came to **protest** unfair treatment of black people. They listened to Dr. Martin Luther King Jr. give a great speech. Over the next few years, there were other protests. Finally, the laws were changed. Since then, people of all races have had the same rights.

Winning Respect

People who live in D.C. did not have the right to vote for president until 1961. Today, the city still does not have voting members in Congress.

This bothers many people who live in Washington, D.C. They work hard. They pay taxes. They serve in wartime. They want to have more of a voice in the laws Congress makes.

Congress has the final word over every law the city passes. Congress controls how much money the city spends. The people who live in Washington, D.C., would like to have more control over their own city.

More than 200,000 people took part in the March on Washington in 1963. They were led by Dr. Martin Luther King Jr. (*center*). Dr. King inspired them with his "I Have a Dream" speech.

IN WASHINGTON, D.C.'S HISTORY

September 11 Attack
Terrorists attacked the United States on September 11, 2001. One of the places they hit is the Pentagon. The Pentagon is in Arlington, Virginia, near Washington, D.C. It is the largest office building in the world. The people who work there are in charge of the nation's defense.

★ ★ ★ Time Line ★ ★ ★

1790	Congress decides to build a new U.S. capital along the Potomac River.
1791	President George Washington picks Pierre L'Enfant to plan the capital.
1800	John Adams is the first president to make his home in the city.
1802	The capital is named the City of Washington.
1814	British troops set fire to the White House and the Capitol. A heavy rainstorm puts out the flames and saves both buildings.
1862	Slavery becomes illegal in Washington, D.C.
1865	President Abraham Lincoln is killed at Ford's Theater.
1884	The Washington Monument is finished.
1922	The Lincoln Memorial is completed.
1963	Martin Luther King Jr. gives his "I Have a Dream" speech at the National Mall.
1982	The Vietnam Veterans Memorial is built.
2001	George W. Bush enters the White House as president. (He starts his second term in 2005.) Terrorists attack the Pentagon in Arlington, Virginia, just outside of Washington, D.C.

People

Today, about 550,000 people live in Washington, D.C. The population was much larger many years ago. Since 1950, people have been moving out of the city. Many have moved to the towns and small cities that have grown up nearby. Now, many more people live in these **suburbs** than in the city.

The city and suburbs form a huge **metropolitan area**. This area includes part of northern Virginia. It includes part of Maryland, too. More than five million

Hispanics: In the 2000 U.S. Census, 7.9 percent of the people living in Washington, D.C., called themselves Latino or Hispanic. Most of them or their relatives came from places where Spanish is spoken. They may come from different racial backgrounds.

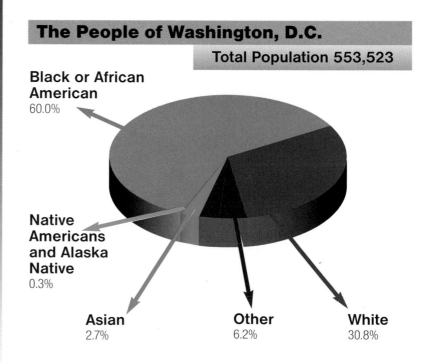

The People of Washington, D.C.

Total Population 553,523

Black or African American
60.0%

Native Americans and Alaska Native
0.3%

Asian
2.7%

Other
6.2%

White
30.8%

Percentages are based on the 2000 Census.

Georgetown is one of the city's most colorful sections. It has many good shops and restaurants. Sunday brunch in Georgetown is a special treat.

people live in D.C. and the nearby suburbs.

Years of Change

The makeup of the city has changed over the years. Before 1950, almost twice as many white people as black people lived there. Today, two blacks live in the city for every white. The reason for this change is simple. Most of the people who left for the suburbs were white.

The city has changed in other ways, too. The number of Hispanics has grown. There are people from almost every country in the world living in the D.C. area. Nearly every country has an **embassy** in Washington, D.C.

The National Cathedral is one of the world's largest churches.

Religion and Education

Most people in the city are Christians. Most of these people are Protestants. Many Roman Catholics live in D.C., too. Jews, Muslims, Hindus, and Buddhists also live here.

For a long time, black children were not allowed to go to the same schools as white children. In 1954, the Supreme Court decided that this was wrong. Now, children of all races go to public schools together.

Washington, D.C., has a small public school system. Some public schools are very good. Other public schools have big problems.

Some parents send their children to private schools.

The city is home to a number of fine colleges and universities. George Washington University is the largest. It has about twenty thousand students. Howard University is also in the city. It opened soon after the Civil War. At that time, black and white students did not usually go to the same colleges. Howard was set up to serve black students. It still attracts many black students. Georgetown is the oldest Catholic university in the nation. It was founded in 1789. Washington, D.C., also is home to Gallaudet University. It is a well-known school for deaf people.

Famous People of Washington, D.C.

Edward Kennedy "Duke" Ellington

Born: April 29, 1899, Washington, D.C.

Died: May 24, 1974, New York, New York

Duke Ellington was a jazz giant. He took piano lessons as a boy. Even so, most of what he learned about music he picked up on his own. As a young man, he often played music for friends at parties. In the 1920s, he put together a band and wrote songs to play. The band went to New York City and started playing at clubs there. By the 1930s, "Duke" was the leader of a world-famous band. One of the band's best-known songs is "Take the 'A' Train."

The Land

Washington, D.C., is small. The city has a land area of only 61 square miles (158 sq km). The amazing thing about D.C. is how much it packs into such a small space.

The city is part of the Atlantic Coastal Plain. Much of D.C. is flat. Swamps have been drained to make more usable land for the city. There are some hills in the northern part of D.C. The highest point in the city is found there. Tenleytown is 410 feet (125 meters) above sea level.

On the Water

The Potomac is the main river. West of the river is Virginia. D.C. is to the east. The Tidal Basin is a small lake linked to the Potomac. On warm, sunny days, people have picnics around the Tidal Basin. They can also rent a paddle boat and go out on the water. The Jefferson Memorial is at the south end of the basin.

The other river in the city is the Anacostia. This river runs through

FUN FACTS

Cherry Blossom Time

Thousands of people visit D.C. each spring. Many come to see the cherry trees in bloom. D.C. has more than 3,700 cherry trees. The first trees were a gift from Japan in 1912. When the trees are in bloom, parts of the city seem to be filled with clouds of pink and white. The Tidal Basin is a good place to see the cherry blossoms. Many cherry trees grow around the Jefferson Memorial. The city has a Cherry Blossom Festival every year.

WASHINGTON, D.C.

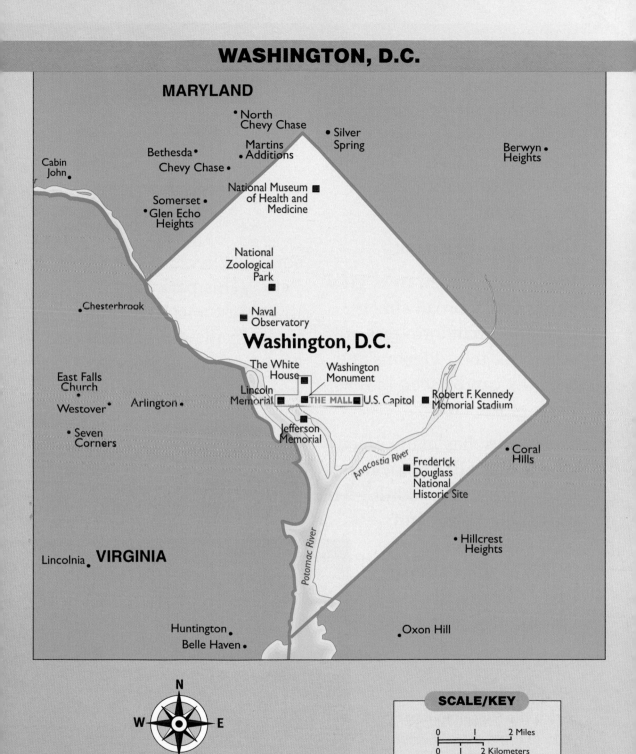

MARYLAND

- North Chevy Chase
- Silver Spring
- Berwyn Heights
- Bethesda
- Martins Additions
- Chevy Chase
- Cabin John
- National Museum of Health and Medicine
- Somerset
- Glen Echo Heights
- National Zoological Park
- Chesterbrook
- Naval Observatory

Washington, D.C.

- The White House
- Washington Monument
- Lincoln Memorial
- THE MALL
- U.S. Capitol
- Robert F. Kennedy Memorial Stadium
- East Falls Church
- Westover
- Arlington
- Jefferson Memorial
- Seven Corners
- Coral Hills
- Anacostia River
- Frederick Douglass National Historic Site
- Lincolnia **VIRGINIA**
- Hillcrest Heights
- Potomac River
- Huntington
- Belle Haven
- Oxon Hill

N W E S

SCALE/KEY

0 1 2 Miles

0 1 2 Kilometers

much of southern D.C. It flows into the Potomac. Trash and sewer waste have polluted the water. The city is trying to make the river clean again.

Going for the Green

Poplar and linden trees grow along D.C.'s broad streets. Oak and sycamore trees are common, too. Pigeons and seagulls can be seen in most parts of the city.

The city has many green places that offer homes to birds and other wildlife. The great blue heron and bald eagle nest on the banks of the Potomac River. Foxes, deer, chipmunks, and

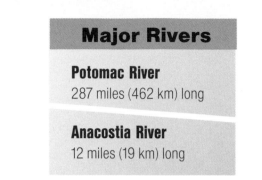

Major Rivers

Potomac River
287 miles (462 km) long

Anacostia River
12 miles (19 km) long

squirrels live in Rock Creek Park. This park is one of the oldest and largest city parks in the world. It is one of the greenest spots in D.C.

Sections of the City

At the heart of Washington, D.C., stands the Capitol. The Capitol is where

From the Potomac River you can get a clear view of Georgetown University.

Congress meets. West of the Capitol is a broad area called the National Mall. This area has many museums.

The rest of the city is divided into four main sections. These are the Northwest, the Northeast, the Southeast, and the Southwest. The Northwest is the largest section. The Southwest is the smallest.

Visitors to D.C. usually spend most of their time in the Northwest. This area is next to the Potomac River. The White House is located there. So are Rock Creek Park and the National Zoo. The Georgetown area is also in the Northwest. Georgetown has many fine shops. It also has good places to eat.

FUN FACTS

Come to the Zoo!

Just south of Rock Creek Park is the National Zoo. The zoo has many unusual animals. Many people go to see the giant pandas. They are on loan from China. The zoo had exciting news in 2005. In July, one of its pandas gave birth to a cub. The cub was no bigger than a stick of butter!

Many people come to the National Zoo to see the giant pandas from China.

Economy

Government is a very big business in Washington, D.C. Some people work for the city government. Many more have jobs in the **federal government**. Federal workers have important jobs. Some of them defend the country against enemies. Others solve crimes. They deliver mail. They collect taxes. They test foods and medicines to make sure they are safe.

The federal government spends huge sums of money. Much of this money is

The White House is where the president lives and works. Visitors come here from all over the world.

paid to businesses that are in the D.C. area. Some of the businesses provide housing, food, and clothing. Others print newspapers, books, magazines, and even laws. Some businesses offer advice to the government. They try to affect the laws passed by Congress.

Visitors Welcome

Tourism is the city's second-largest industry. Millions of people visit the city every year. Some come to D.C. on business. Others come for fun. Visitors are good for the D.C. economy. They rent cars. They take planes and trains. They ride in taxis. They stay in hotels. They eat at restaurants. They pay money for other services. The money they spend means jobs for many people in the D.C. area.

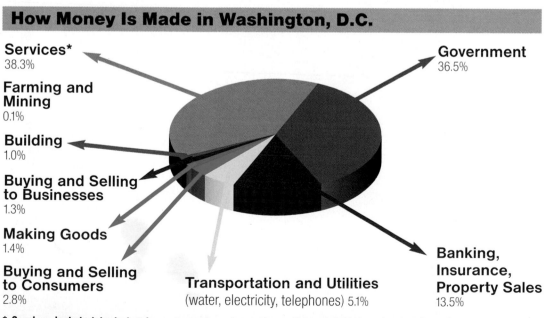

How Money Is Made in Washington, D.C.

Services*
38.3%

Farming and Mining
0.1%

Building
1.0%

Buying and Selling to Businesses
1.3%

Making Goods
1.4%

Buying and Selling to Consumers
2.8%

Government
36.5%

Banking, Insurance, Property Sales
13.5%

Transportation and Utilities
(water, electricity, telephones) 5.1%

* Services include jobs in hotels, restaurants, auto repair, medicine, teaching, and entertainment.

23

Government

Washington, D.C., has its own government. This government has three parts. These parts are the executive, legislative, and judicial branches. The federal government has a big say in how the city is run.

Executive Branch

Every four years, people in D.C. vote for a mayor. The mayor heads the city's executive branch. This branch carries out the city's laws.

Anthony Williams is the mayor of Washington, D.C. He heads the city's executive branch.

Five deputy mayors help the mayor. They are part of the mayor's **cabinet**.

Legislative Branch

People who live in D.C. elect a city council. The council makes the laws for the city. Even so, Congress has the final say over all laws the council passes. Congress also decides how much money the city can spend.

Judicial Branch

The judicial branch includes judges and courts. They may decide whether people who have been accused of committing crimes are guilty. The U.S. president chooses all the judges. The **Senate** then votes on the people the president chooses.

WASHINGTON, D.C., CITY GOVERNMENT

Executive		Legislative		Judicial	
Office	Length of Term	Body	Length of Term	Court	Length of Term
Mayor	4 years	Council (13 members)	4 years	Appeals (9 judges)	15 years
				Superior (87 judges)	15 years

Things to See and Do

The National Mall has many great museums. They are a part of the Smithsonian Institution. One museum is full of airplanes and rockets. Another museum has dinosaur bones on display. Yet another museum focuses on Native Americans. These are just a few of the museums on the Mall.

Famous Places

The White House is the home of the president's family, called the First Family. The president works here. The president's staff works here, too.

A statue in D.C. shows a former president, Franklin D. Roosevelt. Next to him is a statue of his dog Fala.

The Congress meets at the Capitol. The Capitol dome was finished in 1863. Today, the dome is one of the city's best-known sights.

The Supreme Court is the nation's highest court. The nine members of the court meet at the Supreme Court Building. This building stands near the Capitol.

History Lessons

The city is a great place to learn about U.S. history. At the west end of the Mall is the Lincoln Memorial. It has a statue of Abraham Lincoln. From there, visitors have a clear view of the Washington Monument. This tall white building was named for the first U.S. president. It is the tallest building in the city.

Memories of War

Some monuments honor U.S. soldiers who died in

Each year, the president and the First Family light the National Christmas Tree.

wars. A big monument on the Mall deals with **World War II**. It honors the many thousands of Americans who were killed in that war. The Vietnam Veterans Memorial is a simple black stone wall. Carved on the wall are the names of 58,000 Americans who lost their lives during the Vietnam War.

Sports

Football is a popular sport in Washington, D.C. Many fans root for the Washington Redskins. This team won the Super Bowl three times in ten years.

They play at FedEx Field in Maryland.

RFK Stadium hosts many sports events. A pro soccer team, called the D.C. United, plays at this stadium. The Washington Nationals play baseball at RFK, too. They hope to move to a new ballpark in 2008.

Fans head to the MCI Center for indoor sports. The Washington Wizards play men's basketball here. The Washington Mystics women's team plays there, too. The city's pro hockey

Ronald Reagan was president in the 1980s. In this photo, Reagan and his wife Nancy visit the Vietnam Veterans Memorial.

team is the Washington Capitals.

Music and More

Top actors, dancers, and musicians often appear at the Kennedy Center. The MCI Center is another good place to hear music. Pop, rock, and rap stars perform there. City festivals also have good music. The D.C. Blues Festival is held each year. In the fall, the National Zoo hosts a Latin music festival.

Christmas is a festive time. The president and the First Family light the National Christmas Tree.

Major league baseball returned to D.C. in 2005. The Nationals are the city's home team.

FUN FACTS

Batter Up!
Washington, D.C., did not have a major league baseball team for more than thirty years. Baseball came back to the city in 2005. That really gave fans in D.C. something to cheer about!

This very tall Colorado blue spruce tree stands near the White House. Another giant tree is lit at the Capitol.

cabinet — the team that helps the chief executive

capital — the city where the government of a state or country is located

Capitol — the building where Congress meets

colonies — groups of people living in a new land but being controlled by the place they came from

Congress — the part of the U.S. government that makes the laws

embassy — an office run by one country in the capital of another country

federal government — the government of the United States

metropolitan area — a city and its suburbs

monuments — statues or buildings that honor famous people or events

protest — to speak out against something

Senate — one of the two houses of the U.S. Congress

suburbs — the settled areas around a city

surveyed — made a detailed study

Vietnam War — a war fought by U.S. soldiers in Asia from 1964 to 1973

White House — the building where the U.S. president lives and works

World War II — a war fought by U.S. soldiers in Europe and the Pacific from 1941 to 1945

Books

George Washington. Rookie Biographies (series). Wil Mara (Children's Press)

A Kid's Guide to the White House: Is George Washington Upstairs? Betty Debnam (Andrews McMeel)

Martin Luther King and the March on Washington. All Aboard Reading (series). Frances E. Ruffin (Grosset & Dunlap)

Washington, D.C. Rookie Read-About Geography (series). Simone T. Ribke (Children's Press)

Web Sites

Congress for Kids
www.congressforkids.net/

National Zoo — Giant Pandas
nationalzoo.si.edu/Animals/GiantPandas/

Smithsonian Education — Students Home Page
www.smithsonianeducation.org/students

Washington Nationals
washington.nationals.mlb.com

White House Kids Home Page
www.whitehouse.gov/kids/

Adams, John 9
African Americans 11,
  14–15
American Red Cross 10
Anacostia River 18, 20
Arlington 12
Atlantic Coastal Plain 18

Banneker, Benjamin 8
Barton, Clara 10
Booth, John Wilkes 11
Bush, George W. 13

Capitol building 8–10,
  20–21, 27, 29
cherry blossoms 18
Christmas 27, 29
civil rights movement
  11, 12
Civil War, U.S. 9–11, 17
Congress, U.S. 8, 11–12,
  23, 25

economy 22–23
education 16–17
Ellington, Duke 17
embassies 15

Ford's Theater 11

geography 18–21
Georgetown 15, 21
Georgetown University
  17, 20

George Washington
  University 17
government 22–25
Great Britain 6–9

Hispanics 14, 15
Howard University 17

Jefferson Memorial 4, 18

Kennedy Center for the
  Performing Arts 29
King, Martin Luther, Jr.
  11, 12

Lin, Maya 27
Lincoln, Abraham 9–11
Lincoln Memorial 13, 27

museums 21, 26
music 17, 29

National Cathedral 16
National Christmas Tree
  27, 29
National Mall 11, 21,
  26–28
National Zoo 21, 29
Native Americans 6–7,
  14, 26

Pentagon 12
Piscataway (Native
  group) 6–7
population 5, 14

Potomac River 6, 8, 18,
  20, 21

Reagan, Nancy 28
Reagan, Ronald 28
religion 16
Revolutionary War 7
RFK Stadium 28
Rock Creek Park 20, 21
Roosevelt, Franklin D. 26

September 11, 2001,
  terrorist attacks 12
slaves and slavery 8–10
Smith, John 6
Smithsonian Institution
  26
sports 28–29
Supreme Court, U.S.
  16, 27

Vietnam Veterans
  Memorial 13, 27, 28
voting rights 11–12

War of 1812 8–9
Washington, George 8, 9
Washington Monument
  13, 27
White House 9, 21, 22,
  26
Williams, Anthony 24
World War II 28